POLITICIANS FROM HELL

: An Essay on the Politics of Poverty

Professor David P Gregg
(retired)

Politicians From Hell
Published by Green Man Books 2015
15 Poulton Green Close, Spital, Wirral
CH63 9FS (davidgregg@ talktalk.net)

ISBN 978-1507610275

Printed By Create Space
Available from Amazon, the author
and other retail outlets

I was poor so you made me poorer. I was disabled so you called me a benefit cheat. I could not find work so you called me a scrounger. My child was hungry so you called me a bad parent. My mind was broken so you made me a criminal.

For the 'undeserving poor' of Britain

POLITICIANS FROM HELL

'Totalitarian regimes know that human beings need a high degree of certainty if they are to lead happy and free lives. Such regimes therefore organise themselves to deny such certainty, knowing that its absence makes it that much easier to control and subject the populace.'

Neighbours From Hell; Frank Field MP

Readers should remember the above statement as we proceed. It underlines our theme. As the 2015 general election approached we saw desperate attempts, by the three established parties, to demonise the candidates of UKIP, as 'fruit cakes' and 'nut cases'. This can be seen as part of the legitimate, democratic examination of those who would represent us. This process is legitimate so long as the attitudes and views of their own MPs and parliamentary candidates are also open to public scrutiny. The public surely needs to be informed about all the fruitcakes, whatever their party. Indeed, it would be greatly beneficial to democracy if we could look in detail at the 'real' thinking of all the candidates. Sadly this is only sometimes possible.

In this spirit of openness let us examine the words, deeds and character of Frank Field, MP for Birkenhead, who has often shared his political thoughts very 'frankly', unlike many of his colleagues. We will also compare Frank's views with the public remarks of Conservative ministers and find interesting convergences.

Frank has the unique distinction of having both his major reviews of welfare and poverty policy, commissioned by Tony Blair and David Cameron, at far ends of the nominal political spectrum, quietly ignored by the sponsors themselves. Yet Frank, it is said, is widely regarded as an independent, principled, good, indeed almost saintly, chap who it must be accepted, has occasionally produced some good ideas. For example in 2014 Frank led the study into hunger in the UK, producing the well received report, 'Feeding Britain'. His all party team took evidence on the role of poverty, low wages, benefit delays, cuts and sanctions, and so on, in creating hunger in British families. All these hunger factors had already been widely flagged by experts and activists for some years and denied by politicians in power, but another public airing was useful.

As to solutions, in addition to wage and benefit reform, the team also pointed to the shameful waste of edible supermarket food which could be given to the poor, perhaps via state enhanced food banks. So far so good.

However with politicians like Frank there is no such thing as a free lunch. Frank, arguably, had a very old personal axe to grind and presumably found a like minded team to go along with him. Frank emphasised family 'resilience' as a hunger creating factor: basically that some poor families created their own hunger problems through ignorance or deliberate irresponsibility. At the press launch of the report, the posh Tory, Lady Jenkin, told us that the problem was that many poor families did not know how to cook cheap food. She herself recommended porridge! This position was widely seen by the public and media commentators as 'blaming the victims'. Lady Jenkin was forced to withdraw her derogatory comments but correctly pointed out that she was only repeating what was in Frank's report, as agreed by the team. Frank wisely, kept his head down and let Jenkin take the flak. In fact the report quite sensibly recommends the inclusion of parenting, cooking and budgeting lessons for all, in the National Curriculum, to train our future parents…sensible, providing Frank has nothing to do with defining those lessons, for reasons which will become clear.

However, the report also points to inadequate and irresponsible parents who waste their meagre incomes on selfish non-essentials and let their children go hungry. These wicked, undeserving poor should be sent to the 'Troubled Families Projects' for social reprogramming, according to Frank's report. Let's look at the implications of this proposal, which the media missed.

These projects, we are told by the Department for Communities & Local Government, are for 'chaotic' families who are responsible for 'most of the crime and antisocial behaviour in the UK' and who cost the state a fortune to support. In the projects they will face 'assertive, non-negotiable interventions' and 'tough sanctions'. In fact these projects began under Tony Blair as a 'treatment' for antisocial behaviour but for fifteen years they targeted poor, jobless, underclass families with serious physical and mental health problems who often had disabled children, council rent arrears, dirty homes and untidy gardens. Only a very small proportion had criminal records. We are repeatedly told by Eric Pickles, the C&LG minister, that they should all feel 'shame' and 'guilt', presumably for being inadequate and ill… and for costing the state money. Eric has called for a 'less understanding' approach and instructed councils to 'confront' the families and force them to 'take responsibility', adding

—

'We have sometimes run away from categorising, stigmatising, laying blame…It's time to wake up to that …to realise the state is no longer willing to subsidise a life of complete non-fulfilment on just about every level'

Eric's big idea, following the Summer Riots, was to evict whole families from social housing if a youngster misbehaved. We will see that Frank has been pushing this same nostrum for many years.

Contrary to successive government claims, the lives of most of these feckless families were not 'turned around' in the projects. How do we know that? Well apart from several formal, government sponsored evaluations, we have the word of the woman who supervised the programme for over a decade. Louise Casey CB, was Tony Blair's ASBO Tsar and then Respect Tsar and is now Cameron's Troubled Families Tsar. On the 12.06.14 Casey made a speech at a meeting of the Reform organisation and told us

'As hard as it is to accept, the truth is despite our best efforts over many years -and I include myself in that- we just haven't got it right. We haven't succeeded in getting these families to change or in stopping the transmission of problems from generation to generation – we just haven't'

But in public she was still telling the press that

'We are not running some cuddly social workers programme…we should be better at talking about things like shame and guilt…we have lost the ability to be judgemental because we worry about being seen as nasty to poor people'

Indeed; the projects relied on assertive, non-negotiable interventions and tough sanctions: the modern politician's equivalent of stoning to cast out devils. At the same time the Children's Society was reporting that

'Vast numbers of the country's vulnerable families are being left without help, trapped in desperate conditions, struggling with unemployment, disability, poor quality housing and in urgent need of support'

What the projects did do was put the mark of Cain on these unfortunate, vulnerable families. Around 60% were subsequently hounded out of their homes by vigilantes. These are the projects to which Frank wants to send the non-criminal, but inadequate families identified in his Hunger report. Perhaps they can be bullied out of starvation and malnutrition, although fifteen years of evidence says not.

We will see that Frank has long had these inadequate families of the 'undeserving poor' in his sights as part of his grand plan to rebuild UK society in his own image. But if Frank is so respected by fellow politicians why are his major policy ideas not implemented more often? In fact his ideas are influential but often are not to be acknowledged publicly, as the Lady Jenkin 'porridge' fiasco demonstrated. A detailed analysis of all Frank's policy adventures is beyond the scope of a short essay and would be too technical for most tastes, but here is what Tony Blair said about Frank's work in his own autobiography

'The problem was not so much that his thoughts were unthinkable as unfathomable'

It is true that Frank, on occasion, suffers from explanatory dyslexia in his writings but the author contends that the core problem remains that when Frank does speak clearly there is much to be afraid of, whether thoughtful voter or nominally democratic politician. Let us take as the classical example Frank's master work, 'Neighbours From Hell: the Politics of Behaviour', 2003, which was written before caution about publicly expressing his more 'interesting' views set in.

I highly recommend this book to anyone interested in how a democratic society should conduct itself… and how it should not. It is as relevant now as we endure austerity and the poor and sick are stigmatised by the state, as it was then. In essence in NFH, Frank paints an apocalyptic picture of the decay of British society and its decline into a 'social abyss' under the assault of the 'semi-barbarian hordes'. He builds on the hysteria of the New Labour ASBO Jihad and then utilises this dark vision to justify his model of invasive, state, social control mechanisms. Frank tells us calmly that

'Antisocial behaviour is on the march…[it] is the new horseman of the apocalypse… [it] is nothing less than a war for civilisation as we know it…
 The measures the [New Labour] government has taken …will not contain the new nihilists, let alone **strike down** their recruiting sergeants'

Who are these recruiting sergeants? They appear to be the religious 'doubters' who follow the Enlightenment idea of the 'moral autonomy of man' and who insist to Frank that 'my views are just as good as yours'. This Frank will not tolerate. We will see that he intends to 'strike down' such godless dissenters by excluding them from public debate. As we proceed many readers may detect a whiff of the Taliban or possibly of Soviet Russia. See what you think.

And if the reader thinks Frank's apocalyptic visions have faded over the years, note that in late 2014 he told the local press that his constituency, Birkenhead, was

'becoming like Beirut!'

This hyperbole was at odds with the facts on the Wirral council ASB website. Here we find that the number of ASB incidents in 2014 was the same as in 2008 and lower than in the years before that. But then a general election was coming: time to frighten the electorate again and win votes! It worked for Tony Blair after all. By January 2015 as the election warmed up, Frank was out on the streets of 'Beirut' (with a TV crew) hunting a 'fast' moving 'yob gang'…so fast they could not be found! His sound bite solution : new legislation 'that warmly shakes them by the throat'. Yes, let's bring back hanging, or maybe beheading, Taliban style? Actually Frank we have masses of law, thanks to New Labour, which does not seem to have helped. What we need are evidence-based intervention strategies, not sound bites. What we need are more police, freed from New Labour paperwork, and out on the streets combating real crime and disorder. And surely Frank knows we already have the powerful, Coalition introduced, Gang Injunctions and the Injunction to Prevent Nuisance and Annoyance which is even more draconian than the old ASBO? Perhaps he really does want public beheading? If it's good enough for our close allies, the Saudis, why not?

Let's begin our look at NFH with Frank's ASBO fear spin in 2004. He sells his national apocalypse thesis with local anecdotes. Let's compare his numbers with the above Birkenhead is 'Beirut' claim. We read that in Wirral there are 5 households which ambulances will not attend without a police presence because the families have a reputation for 'brawling'. Frank does not claim ambulance staff were ever assaulted only that such assault was a 'possibility'. If these 5 families did assault medical staff, who they themselves had called for help, surely this would signal a significant mental health problem requiring investigation? And is Frank really unaware that in this 'Health & Safety' obsessed country ambulance staff are instructed not to attend homes, for example, with dementia sufferers without a police escort because of the 'possibility' of a violent reaction?

By the way, given the Wirral population, Frank's 5 families represent ~0.01% of households. If we accept Frank's valid point that the 'families from hell' are concentrated in the poorest communities, let us say the poorest 10%, we can increase this to a ~ 0.1% frequency. Other data confirm this scale. Frank tells of a 'respectable area of terraced housing' of some 300 homes 'quickly decimated' by just two 'dysfunctional' families. That is an incidence of 0.67%.

The British Crime Survey of experience and perceptions of antisocial behaviour, which Frank trusts, tells us that in 2003 / 4 only ~2% of people believed that neighbour disputes were a 'very big' problem.

Frank, master of understatement, describes these few problem families as the 'new horsemen of the apocalypse'(By the way the major 'anti-social behaviour problems' in the BCS report were said to be speeding cars at 43%; inconsiderately parked cars at 31% ; litter at 29%. At 28% we have 'teenagers hanging around' ...not causing trouble, just being there. In the full report we learn that only 3% of respondents had experienced an actual problem with such teenagers hanging around).

The distress caused by the small number of 'dysfunctional' families should not be marginalised, but the issue is how best to deal with them in order to protect the public effectively. Frank himself tells us that the police have an arsenal of law to deal with criminal behaviour and that they should use it. We also have the broadly applicable and effective Harassment Act. However Frank points us to the impact of non-criminal, low level serial 'annoyance' by youngsters and the need to combat that. The New Labour nostrum for this problem was the ASBO which abandoned the ancient principle of a universal common law and invented tailor made, one off, personalised offences while allowing anonymous and hearsay evidence in court and public denigration of accused adults and children before trial or a right to reply. The use of the magic spell, 'behaviour causing or likely to cause harassment, alarm or distress', by the complainant was sufficient. Whether such a response was objectively justified was never tested. Nor was it necessary any longer to show intent or mens rea, guilty mind, in the accused. **98%** of ASBO applications, mostly by council ASBO teams and housing officers, were granted. A five year prison sentence could be given for breaching an order originally issued for behaviour that was not criminal. It was like shooting fish in a barrel. In fact the council in Frank's constituency won a prize for its catchy and sadly accurate public slogan

'Abuse your rights; Loose your rights'

There is much to be said about the dangerous legal precedents set by the ASBO for all of us but the key point is that it was a failure. ASBO breach rates reached 70% in England and 35% were breached 5 or more times. In some cities like Manchester the breach rate was 90%. Frank wants more of the same failed medicine. In court it was found that over 60% of those accused had diagnosed mental health problems and learning disabilities, according to the Cabinet Office in 2002. God knows how many went undiagnosed. The process went for the low hanging fruit, not the real yobs and criminals.

The ASBO was quickly abandoned in Scotland, Northern Ireland and Eire as the courts and police absorbed the performance evidence. In New Labour England & Wales the ineffective farce continued until they were thrown out.

Frank himself proudly played a role in the criminalisation of non-criminal behaviour by young children.

'I believed that the law should be changed so that by merely committing certain designated acts, a person was deemed old enough to be held accountable for those actions. This proposal… was seen into law in the Crime and Disorder Act 1998.'

This and other innovations eliminated the ancient common law principle of doli incapax which held that children of ten could not be considered legally responsible. These New Labour innovations, as their impacts on children became clear, including a huge increase in criminalisation, were condemned by the four home Children's Commissioners, various parliamentary committees, the Human Rights Commissioner of the Council of Europe and the UN Children's Commissioner. Well done Frank.

Note that it is well established in modern neurology that the right temporo-parietal junction area of the brain dealing with higher decision making and 'moral' judgements does not physically complete its development until the early twenties. In some it never fully develops. The brain is a purely physical organ and a very vulnerable one. Experiments show that using trans-cranial magnetic stimulation of the RTPJ it is possible to disrupt 'moral' judgements in normal people. It would be interesting to try this on Frank and other moralising politicians. Of course judging by the scale of the ongoing MP expenses, cash for influence and Westminster paedophile ring scandals, some may already have damage in that brain area. Childhood behavioural problems are also strongly linked to poor nutrition. Abnormal neurology and malnutrition are crucial here, not moral degeneracy.

After New Labour was thrown out, the police and courts recovered their backbones and sanity. The number of arrests of children fell from 315,923 in 2008 to 209,450 in 2011, a fall of 37%. However 2,117 children of 10 or 11 were still arrested in 2011 so Frank's law is still in play in some places. The Howard League for Penal Reform said

'A commitment to public safety means treating them as vulnerable children and making sure they get the help they need to mature into law-abiding citizens.'

We will see that this needed help is often medical and nutritional. Similarly a senior Metropolitan Police spokesman also commented on the data

'We are not chasing [New Labour] targets anymore. We have realised that once children get arrested and get involved with the criminal justice system they are likely to offend again and that is what we want to avoid at all costs'

Well done Frank, but by all means ignore the experts and the facts. In fact Frank's influential 'war against children' reached a point where it became 'legal' and 'patriotic' to deploy a 'low level sonic weapon', the Mosquito device, in public places. These devices put out an indiscriminate wall of high frequency sound painful to teenagers, children and babies, aimed at 'moving them on' from outside shops and council facilities. Several thousand were installed despite warnings from the Children's Commissioners and the Council of Europe Human Rights Commissioner. A later Mosquito version was frequency tuneable to stop the adult homeless sleeping in doorways. We should all be very proud.

This brings us to the issue of the causation of low level antisocial behaviour and chaotic families, the understanding of which, is surely central to tackling them effectively. We will find later that Frank sees the problem in terms of moral degeneracy in the underclass and the solution in terms of imposing a substitute for evangelical Christianity while introducing pervasive state controls including welfare sanctions, suppression of public discourse and the silencing of the 'recruiting sergeants of nihilism'.

Meanwhile here are a few actual facts about the youngsters and families caught up in the ASBO Jihad and 'Troubled Families Projects' which might hint at more effective strategies. Some 60 – 80% of those receiving ASB interventions were found to have serious mental / physical health problems and learning disabilities. This was known in the early 2000s by the New Labour government and ignored. There were more votes in the yob and families from hell narratives. In 2012 the Children's Commissioner brought together all the evidence and published 'Nobody Made the Connection: the prevalence of neurological deficits in young offenders'. The report compared the prevalence of mental health disorders in young offenders and the general population with remarkable results.

The prevalence of general learning disability (IQ < 70) in young offenders is **9.2 X** that in the general population.

The prevalence of autistic spectrum disorders is **16.6 X** higher.

The prevalence of communication disorders (Torretes, etc) is **12.5 X** higher.

The prevalence of dyslexia is **5 X** higher.

The prevalence of ADHD is **2.5 X** higher.

We can add another statistic from repeated surveys by Mencap and Mind: people with such disorders are **8 X** more likely to suffer regular physical and verbal abuse in their communities. They are often abused and then scapegoated, taking the blame in local disputes and being unable to explain themselves to the authorities. By the way these mentally disordered people are then **9 X** more likely to die in police custody than normal folks. But as Frank compassionately tells us in NFH

'If a drunk can fight there is little chance of them dying from their own vomit'

People die because the police often cannot tell the difference between a drunk and somebody who is mentally ill or learning disabled and, actually Frank, it is perfectly possible for a drunk or a mentally disordered person to panic on arrest, thrash about and then collapse, particularly after a beating. Ask a doctor. As Frank tells us, 'his' ASB is often about serial 'annoyance' and sadly it is true that living near neighbours with mental disorders may be challenging, or worrying but does that warrant, moralising denigration and criminalisation, rather than medical intervention?

Having considered evidence about causation let us look in more detail at Frank's solution approach, based on his moral degeneracy hypothesis.

'Neighbours from Hell's central thesis is a consideration of what can replace the largely beneficial role evangelical Christianity once played in moulding civilised behaviour'.

According to Frank, lacking Christianity and hence a Victorian respect for 'authority' figures such as priests and politicians, the modern parents of the underclass have failed to teach their children their proper place. The ASB problem lies then, in bad, godless, parenting among the poor.

He also addresses the question of poverty in an interesting historical way.

'The liberation from the Victorian approach – **or so it is interpreted** – came when the poverty debate began laying the blame for poverty on society and its institutions, instead of the poor themselves... the more recently established conventional wisdom is that poverty is caused by lack of money and not by the behaviour of the poor.'

Frank obviously sees the bad behaviour of the poor as central, as he is still promoting in Feeding Britain, but so that he cannot be accused (as a nominally Labour MP) of 'poor bashing' Frank makes a distinction between the deserving poor who toe the line, live within their means and plan ahead for their old age, the people who 'put on their best clothes to visit their MP', as opposed to the undeserving poor among whom we find the feckless, bad parents and their children who cause antisocial behaviour : parents who choose to let their children starve.

Why do these groups differ? Frank has his answer ready:

'How can these different circumstances be explained if personal character and its view of responsibility are written out of the script?'

Poverty it seems is often simply a matter of poor moral character and lack of personal responsibility! Mental and physical ill heath, learning disability and social inadequacy do not come into it despite the extensive evidence. Frank equates the undeserving, feckless poor with his deviant families from hell, a distinct antisocial minority, nothing to do with their decent, respectable neighbours. Is this true? Well Sheffield Hallam University produced a series of 'ASBO Sin Bin' project evaluations for the New Labour government, still cited by the Coalition. This research group summarised their extensive experience of the families from hell in a number of published papers.

'Contrary to popular belief the evidence suggests that rather than being a distinct minority, families tended to conform to the norms and values of the communities in which they lived'

How could this possibly be? Well the researchers were clear as to why the problem families differed

'The subjects of ASB interventions often have mental health problems, learning disabilities and neurological disorders. This raises the crucial question about the use of punitive control mechanisms. ASBOs in particular may serve to exacerbate their problems'

Exacerbating mental disorders surely does not improve the protection of the public. So Frank is on the wrong causation track but he helpfully goes further in his analysis.

'If the absence of an ability simultaneously to weigh the needs of others with ones own priorities is the first defining characteristic of antisocial individuals, a second defining characteristic is that they do not see any value, or relevance in looking beyond the now in calculating the consequences of their actions. Thinking through the longer term consequences of their behaviour is simply an **unintelligible activity.** ...As an ever greater number of families become dysfunctional an ever increasing supply of **socially offensive individuals** results'

Frank has put his finger on important causative factors here but wrongly assigns them to a moral dimension. But many of the mental disorders we looked at earlier, which are far more frequently encountered in those accused of antisocial behaviour and bad parenting, are characterised by low IQs and cognitive executive dysfunctions, namely: disinhibition; impulsivity; lack of ability to compute consequences of actions and 'plan ahead'; inability to put themselves in other's shoes; inability to control involuntary behaviours which may cause alarm or offence; inability to understand complex social situations and instructions; inability to explain events to others ; anxiety, depression and consequent aggression. The frequency of such disorders in the population is steady over time but the New Labour government, for its own political purposes, encouraged communities to see people with such disorders, as Frank says, as 'socially offensive'. Where once communities tolerated their village idiots, or set the local bobby on the most annoying, now they are encouraged to send for the council ASBO team: the sub-human rat catchers.

Despite the high and well recognised incidence of mental disorders among the ASBO recipients and the 'families from hell' forced into the 'ASBO Sin Bins', it is remarkable that less than 10% of those on court orders received the Individual Support Orders originally intended to provide mental health and other medical treatment. Only ~12% of 'families from hell' in the 'ASBO Sin Bins' received professional psychiatric treatment or counselling. It is little wonder that the ASBO Jihad failed. It is little wonder that the abusive 'Troubled Family Projects' are still failing as Louise Casey CB, Troubled Families Tsar, told us earlier. Given the above facts, Frank's analysis of causation is clearly faulty and we must therefore be cautious about his proposed solutions. However later in his book, having made the case for his utopian Moral Jihad on the basis of the 'semi-barbarian' flood, Frank suddenly discovers a national survey which examines the reasons why British parents with problems seek outside advice. Frank says

'First, health problems were the most reported reasons for seeking help by parents of children under five. If learning and behavioural difficulties are added together this group then jumps to the second most significant reason given by parents in   difficulties. For older children behavioural problems were the most common issue on which advice was sought…Poorer parents were twice as likely to seek advice, than their working counterparts. The exception was of single mothers at work who reported a higher incidence of problems than non-working families'

So by 'poorer' Frank means non-working and on benefits: the unemployed and the long term ill and disabled. (By the way by 2013 the Centre for Social Justice report 'Signed On: Written Off' found that Birkenhead, Frank's constituency, was fourth in the UK league table for people on 'out of work benefits' with 55% of those aged 16 to 64 in that category). Frank acknowledges that many parents recognise health and behaviour problems in their children and that twice as many of the really poor seek help with such problems. But these include many characterised by Frank as bad parents and neighbours from hell.

The history shows that the chances of such people getting the medical help they, above all others, need is low and continues to be low even after the state has unhelpfully 'intervened' through the criminal justice system. The most likely outcome for inadequate families remains state bullying and criminalisation, not treatment. Why did Frank not mention this important information when he introduced his readers to the 'families from hell' and discussed ASB causation? Well firstly, it might have generated inconvenient compassion for these morally degenerate, 'socially offensive', godless people and secondly, it would have undermined the logic of his sanctions based, social engineering solution.

With all these caveats in mind let us turn in more detail to Frank's political strategy for preventing the social 'apocalypse'. It has three components: firstly respect for important people like Frank 'in authority' must be restored; secondly state benefits for individuals and families should be conditional on 'good behaviour' as defined by Frank of course; thirdly the voices of the 'new nihilists', as defined again by Frank, must not be allowed to influence public debate. Here are Frank's own words beginning with the respect issue:

'Respect is no longer awarded or even conceded simply because a person holds a position [of authority]'

Frank means respect to important people like himself. Not only was he an MP but also a member of the General Synod of the Church of England! Of course respect for MPs and the church is admittedly not what it was but is this due to the moral degeneracy of the people, particularly the godless poor, or the behaviour of the establishment in recent decades: politicians on the gravy train, fiddling expenses and selling influence for money? Is it rather the greedy bankers? Is it the established church long obsessed with internal theological and moral turmoil over women priests, female bishops and gay marriage while the poor and the sick suffered under austerity? Respect should be earned.

Is it any wonder that Christianity in Britain continues to decline? The 2011 census results showed that in the previous decade those professing a nominal Christian faith fell from 72% to 59%. The fraction following no organised religion rose from 15% to 25% in just ten years. Frank no doubt would see these changes as confirming his thesis. However the census also showed that 5.8 million people were caring for sick and disabled family members or friends, a percentage unchanged for a decade. The care provided by the state meanwhile, particularly for the disabled and old, has been in decline for many years, as has social mobility.

Fortunately every year the Children In Need campaign breaks previous records for charitable donations from the public. The public charitable support for food banks has also exploded in the last few years. In 2014 the OECD published a global survey of charitable giving. More than 72% of UK people give to charity every month, well above the average for leading, developed nations. Giving was maintained through the worst recession in a century. Individual compassion, it seems, has survived even as organised religion has declined.

Frank is also clear why respect and **authority must be enforced**: it seems a properly ordered society is a giant 'pyramid selling operation'.

'Such a pyramid sales operation is no bad thing as long as the pyramid continues to be built. Social virtues are practiced because other people practice them. The sense of crisis …stems from an awareness that this gigantic but so beneficial pyramid operation is crumbling'

Is Frank seriously telling us that the 'great social pyramid scam' is crumbling because of a few tens of thousands of dysfunctional, chaotic families at the very bottom of the pile? (Remember in total, New Labour imposed a mere 19,000 ASBOs over thirteen years despite the spin; despite Frank's 'barbarian flood' and apocalypse).

The essence of pyramid selling is that those who set it up, those at the top, make fortunes and those at the bottom take the dregs or nothing. In the last few decades it is those near the top, the bankers and speculators, whose greedy behaviour has damaged the stability of the pyramid, along with the hubris of the senior politicians who were supposed to be its guardians. As the pyramid crumbles it is those at the bottom who will, and are, being crushed: the very poorest, the chronically sick, the disabled, the old. Frank's obsession with imposing respect in the underclass for the likes of him, as a solution to our social and economic ills, is ludicrous. To be fair to Frank he does concede that respect is still sometimes given …but irritatingly, to the wrong sorts.

'Respect can still be awarded. The most obvious recent example here has been Princess Diana. While her good works and general demeanour won her wide respect and affection, **the awarding of respect to this clearly troubled person has more than a whiff of sulphur about it.** What kind of role model does such a troubled figure provide for teenagers and, as importantly, what is the significance of such a choice?'

Frank completely fails to understand that Diana received compassion, if not respect, just because she was 'troubled'. Ordinary people saw their own troubles, their own mental health problems, anxieties, depressions, relationship failures reflected in this tragic 'fairytale' princess. They felt empathy, fellow feeling, compassion. Even Tony Blair understood that. Many of us brought up in the Christian faith might also sense in that spontaneous compassion for a troubled soul, a faint echo of the Christ.

If Frank smells 'more than a whiff of sulphur' in this respect and affection for Diana, it perhaps tells us more about Frank than about a satanically misguided public. But then Frank lives alone in his high tower, unmarried and childless, from which he looks down on the rest of us in righteous judgement as we struggle below to do the best for our families, however inadequately.

He goes on, with his usual understatement, to explain why and how respect and authority must be restored.

'The natural authority that society requires for its proper functioning is being over run by the storm troopers of nihilistic behaviour. It is becoming ever more necessary for that **authority** which is fundamental to the operation of a **free society**, and which was once freely accepted, **to be imposed'**

'**Moral and civic duties** provide the very foundations upon which civilised life is built and are a proper area for **legislative prescription and if necessary sanctions'**

Readers may begin to detect a small disconnect here between a free society and the imposition of Frank's views on morality and enforced authority. When we look at the avalanche of new law and the loss of civil liberties under Tony Blair, Frank's views are perhaps not so far from the New Labour, control freak, mainstream. We must also understand that when Frank talks of state intervention he is thinking big. For example

'Tackling the breakdown of the common decencies culture requires an effort equal to that which is mobilised for war …Just as wars are too important to be left to generals, so parenting is too vital to society's wellbeing to be left to parents unaided'

Generals of course are experienced, often competent, experts. Frank, as an obviously experienced expert in parenting, is going to rebuild the education system in his own image. Teaching the elements of good parenting and indeed citizenship in schools is a sensible innovation so long as unnecessary and ill-founded ideological baggage is not built into the package. As we read on consider whether such baggage could ever be excluded under Frank's model and influence. Recall that Frank is still trying to impose his views on UK education through the Feeding Britain proposals.

The imposition of new authority is to come via 'citizen contracts' and pseudo-religious ceremonies covering all aspects of our lives.

'The new citizen contract would spell out for the first time the duties society places on citizens by linking them to benefit entitlements'

Frank was still pushing citizenship ceremonies in April 2013 at the 'Diversity and White Working Class' conference.

'I think the poor working class in Birkenhead needs them [citizenship ceremonies]…society needs to relearn the rules by which it used to live'

What does this mean? NFH tells us.

'The celebration and registration of the birth of a citizen, the signing of pupil's school contracts, the contracts for drawing income support, housing benefit, incapacity benefit and the like, and the celebratory contract for citizens as they reach the state retirement age, will each offer the community the opportunity to **teach** through the registrar, priest, teacher, trade union official or benefit clerk, what the duties and rights of citizenship involve'

These teaching agents he calls 'enforcement officers'. Just to be clear what Frank means by teaching he also says

'...new boundaries need to be drawn... Benefits provide such a boundary as between them they provide a universal coverage **for those most likely to commit antisocial behaviour'**

Frank has told us that antisocial behaviour and bad parenting are phenomena of the undeserving poor in the underclass but also, that he is not 'poor bashing'. It is interesting then that it is the poorest who will experience Frank's benefit sanctions for behaviour he disapproves of. Remember that in his Birkenhead, 55% of adults depend on out of work benefits, never mind those on working tax credits and the rest.

As Frank received accolades for Feeding Britain remember that this is the thinking behind sending feckless parents to the Troubled Families Projects: we will combat hunger and re-programme the undeserving poor using benefit sanctions if necessary...er, but won't that increase their hunger? Didn't Frank condemn the Coalition in his report for making benefit sanctions and cuts?

The well off, who do not need benefits, are outside such sanctions but in Frank's Utopia they would still suffer the indignity of being lectured about their responsibilities to the state as Frank sees them, by his approved agents: priests, politicians and minor state 'enforcement officers'.

How will such sanctions be enforced in Frank's Utopia?

'The agency deciding what action should follow a repeated failure to meet a [citizen's] contract should be **the police and only the police**. Once the police have the required evidence to levy a sanction, and then lodge that decision, the sanction should automatically come in to operation on the appropriate benefit.'

So the police are to become the only enforcement arm of Frank's Moral Renewal Jihad. The involvement of the police in controlling benefit provision surely makes Frank's fundamental political attitudes and intentions only too plain. What would come next we might wonder?

Well Frank tells us in the third strategic element of his final solution, which is to combat the voices of 'nihilism' in the interests of protecting his idea of a 'free society'. But do not worry dear reader, since

'In no way is Neighbours From Hell advocating **some kind of thought police...** At no point is the aim of NFH to open a window into the minds, thoughts or beliefs of voters... The attempt of critics to occupy the high ground is misplaced for although the new politics is different it is most definitely not about invading the private as opposed to trying to influence what goes on in the public domain'

Yes, in Frank's '1984' Utopia you are free to think what you like ...in private. However

'We enter a different domain when these private views are expressed in public...Private opinions are usually made public with one objective. They are offered in the hope or determination to change the views of other people. Once such opinions are made regularly in a concerted way in public the guardians of our public space have a responsibility to consider the impact on the public peace...If the new politics can be said to be about anything it is how to challenge the **private** views and values which are impacting so adversely on **public** conduct'

Frank will perhaps graciously allow us our private thoughts but not their public expression...if they disagree with Frank's societal model or we lack a position of 'natural authority', such as priest or politician. Who then will be allowed to take part in public debate on issues of concern? Not the man in street. Certainly not the intellectuals and non-Christian doubters who might easily gainsay Frank's arguments and ideas. Is the press to be controlled or is the press allowed to speak as a 'responsible' arm of the metropolitan establishment? Certainly Frank has made wide use of the press to promote his ideas. Can there be a democracy when Frank and his ilk decide who is respectable and responsible enough to be allowed to present their lawful views in public? Taliban indeed.

Frank's position on public discourse is a curious one, given his background. Where would Christianity be if the Christ had declined to give the Sermon on the Mount and taught his creed only in private? European Christianity began in hiding in the catacombs of Rome but despite centuries of persecution, thanks to the bravery of individuals who carried their faith and message into the streets, it conquered an empire.

How could the labour movement or the suffragette movement ever have achieved success if their intellectual leaders and followers had not been able to protest and present their reasoned cases in public? Well, Frank's political party is now at the pinnacle of the establishment and the only way is down. Change, new science and evidence based interpretations of the nature of society and its problems, are to be avoided at all costs. After all they might have facts and reason on their side.

We have looked herein at Frank's magnum opus, Neighbours From Hell, written in 2003 at the height of the ASBO Jihad. However over the years little has changed and Frank is still promoting his repressive model of society as opportunity presents itself. Frank was still berating poor parenting in 2012, claiming that local head teachers would take 20% of their children in to care if they could and that children were starting school 'without knowing their own names' or 'what a book is' and unable 'to dress themselves'. Frank appears unaware that educational policy has long imposed integration of the learning disabled into 'the main stream' while limiting specialist support in schools for such children. He has forgotten that the lowest 0.5% in the IQ distribution, corresponding to the Coalition's 120,000 troubled 'families from hell' reprogramming target, have IQs below 60 points, well below the normal threshold of criminal responsibility in civilised democracies. He has forgotten that studies have repeatedly shown that poor families with mental health, addiction and learning disability problems find it much more difficult to access specialist medical support (even in the ASBO Sins Bins). He has forgotten that the life expectancy of such people is at least a decade shorter than that of the average Briton. He has forgotten that many local authorities have increasingly tried to dodge the issuing of statements of Special Educational Needs because of the long term support cost implications… ASBOs, and now the Coalition 'Injunction to Prevent Nuisance & Annoyance' are much cheaper.

To help the poor, Frank, by 2012, was calling for a tougher cap on housing benefit than even the Coalition government proposed. This is Frank's pattern…the state should always be harsher. Those most affected would be the feckless unemployed with many children …obvious ASBO or IPNA fodder. The issue of profiteering landlords playing the benefits system unchallenged, was not to be loudly condemned, nor the thirteen year long failure of New Labour to build low cost homes. That would only distract from the bad families message.

Frank also returned to his first love, promoted in NFH. In 2002 Frank introduced a parliamentary bill to 'withdraw housing benefit from neighbours from hell'.

Unfortunately his bill failed under the 'time rules' but it seems that the 'Housing Benefit (Withholding of Payment) Bill' was also sabotaged by the parliamentary select committee on human rights who had the temerity to suggest the bill did not comply with the European Convention; the sticking point being the potential suffering of the evicted (poor) family's children. Frank saw all this as the 'defence of unacceptable behaviour'. It is clear that he wants to see the Convention 'rebalanced' or, as we might suspect: gone.

By 2012 with the shortage of social housing, thanks to the neglect of building such housing over many years, Frank again lobbied central and local government via a private members bill to allocate homes on the basis of 'good behaviour' as defined by him in Neighbours From Hell. The problem of course is still that if we refuse a tenancy to a parent and their family because of, let us say, the bad behaviour of a teenage child, is that fair to the other children? This did not stop Eric Pickles proposing the same medicine. But of course bad behaviour is the 'parent's fault' so serve them right and in the New Labour model crime runs in families so all are guilty anyway. If the family is then black listed by Frank's intended sanctions where do they live? In expensive bed and breakfast hostels, paid for by tax payers? Or on the street? Shouldn't we bring back the workhouses favoured by Frank's Victorian Christian, moral paragons?

Frank also helpfully stirred up in the media, the question of 'foreigners' occupying social housing in parallel with his 'good behaviour' campaign. He told us that such foreigners occupied 19% of the social housing in London. Of course London is a very special case. In Frank's own, more typical constituency, the fraction of foreigners and ethnics is less than 3% so it is surprising that this issue is, he says, 'a matter of intense interest in my constituency…'. He told the press that there was

'a strong suspicion that long established citizens have had the rough end of the stick for far too long.'

Frank also told the press recently that if we don't zap immigration and its effects on public services 'it will turn very nasty' in Britain. With rivers of blood perhaps? We can imagine the potential, unfortunate consequences of such rhetoric in some areas of high East European immigration, never mind the areas of Commonwealth Asian immigration. By the way Frank's very own Church Times in November 2008, ran an article by the Bishop of Worcester, on Frank's call to tightly restrict the entry of refugees into Britain. The bishop described the proposals as 'barbaric' and drew a direct comparison with the views of Enoch Powell. Frank does not lack consistency.

Frank is correct to ask for a serious review of allocation policy for social housing but not on the basis of selective statistics, ethnicity, and his NFH sanctions based approach. His nominal party made a complete mess in promoting free for all immigration for ideological reasons, along with their pernicious, 'loony left', multiculturalism policy, but the answer is not rabble rousing. Having set the hounds running Frank then tells us remarkably that

'It is now clear that the relevant statistics are a complete shambles so attempts to reassure them [the voters] can only be based on the most flimsy analysis'

If this is so, these same statistics should surely not be used to create a moral panic, or at worst, xenophobic responses among voters. But this is Frank of course.

In the same month, May 2012, Frank closed the loop on social housing, foreigners, immigration control and dysfunctional, unemployed families by saying

'it's come to a head because I found out that one in five households has never ever had work …the government needs to tell Brussels that we just can't have free movement of labour'

A number of observers who bothered to check found that the real prevalence of perennial non-working homes was not 20% but 1.8%. In fact the DWP recently estimated only ~300,000 households out of ~20 million have never worked or ~1.5%.Frank still has a way with numbers.

By the end of 2012 he was making an all out attack on welfare which he says 'rots the soul'; that is to say welfare creates a moral hazard encouraging bad behaviour among the poor and sick. Presumably it is more preferable for poor families to suffer malnutrition than to risk their souls. But surely this attitude seems a long way from his attack on Coalition welfare cuts in Feeding Britain? As he repeatedly said to the press

'As we **now** have a welfare state based on **meeting need**, this encourages individuals, not unreasonably, to try to ensure they qualify under this guise. It therefore pays to **lie** about one's earnings, to **cheat**, or to **be inactive**. The worst side of human nature is encouraged…'

This is a completely unqualified statement.

It panders, with the authority of a senior MP, to the uninformed sections of society who believe that all welfare recipients are 'benefit cheats' and 'scroungers'. Remember 55% of his own constituents subsist on out of work benefits. In this approach Frank stands with the Coalition. In fact Frank also says on his website that adopting his harsh welfare policy views

'Will put the [labour] party firmly in line with public opinion'

Er...does all this sound like the Saint Frank of the Feeding Britain initiative, as reported by the media? The author is unaccountably reminded, in all this cant, of Dickens' England.

'Oh God, to hear the insect on the leaf pronounce upon the excess life among his hungry brothers in the dust!'
The Spirit of Christmas Present.

As we might expect by now the facts on cheating do not support the propaganda, nor the opinions of the uninformed to whom Frank appeals. In 2012 Lord Freud (the former banker and Blair welfare guru) told parliament that in the last year 'fraud and error' cost the tax payer £3.2 billion. He neglected to say that this amounted to ~2% of the annual welfare bill. Nor did he remind the House and the public that 2 / 3 of this was due to DWP and other administrative error, not fraud. So the benefit cheating rate is ~0.65%, or on a people basis, 1 in 150 benefit recipients.

Let's have a quick look at Lord Freud to compare his interesting views with Frank's. This is what he told the House political magazine recently

'We have got circumstances now where people who are poorer should be prepared to take risks- **they've got the least to loose. I think we have a dreadful welfare system.** You know, the incapacity benefits, the lone parents ...- all kinds of areas where **poor people** are able to have a lifestyle on benefits and actually off **conditionality**'

Conditionality is a favourite Frank word. In 2008 as the Purnell 'reforms' came in, when Freud was 'with' New Labour, he had also said

'We can't have people simply loafing about ...expecting the state to finance their lifestyles. That is the way to the destruction of our society'

Of course by 2012, 60% of the children in poverty were in working families...but let's not bother with the facts.

And Freud was at least consistent. By 2014 he had discovered the disabled. At a Conservative Party Conference fringe event, he told the audience

'…there is a group and I know exactly who you mean, where actually as you say, they [the disabled] are not worth the full [minimum] wage. …I'm going to think about that issue…if someone [disabled] wants to work for £2 per hour'

As food bank usage grew to over half a million Freud also told the House of Lords that welfare 'reforms' and hunger did not cause food banks, rather, opening food banks encouraged scrounging, people to use them. Oxfam spoke for many.

'These comments do not bare much relation to reality. The evidence is very clear that people are going to food banks out of real need'

Freud was widely accused of not understanding the effect of his cuts and sanctions on the already very poor. His considered response was

'You don't have to be a corpse to go to a funeral'

It is hard to properly respond to Freud and his keeper, Iain Duncan Smith. We simply note that David Cameron et al, hold the view that the richest must be given their bonuses and tax breaks to motivate them to work harder **but** the poorest and sickest must have money taken off them to motivate them back into work. Politicians from Hell? Yes.

Let's get back to the evidence about benefit cheating as ignored by Freud et al. From time to time governments have had a populist blitz on 'cheating' but don't always publicise the embarrassing results. The Coalition soon introduced the 'Fraud Hotline' to encourage good citizens to report the cheats. After great efforts they caught 32,000 people. In terms of all those claiming benefits this is again ~0.6%. Recently the benefits police went after those receiving Disability Living Allowance, often among our most needy, disabled people. After extensive investigations they established a cheating rate of less than 0.5%. The equivalent fraud rate on Incapacity Benefit was 0.3%. The evidence seems clear enough… too clear to be broadcast to the public. It might make it more difficult to justify cutting benefits to the poor employed and unemployed, chronically sick and disabled. Under Coalition austerity all the poor are undeserving, but at least the Coalition is not after their souls.

Frank Field was also part of a movement in 2012-13, led by the Coalition, to rewrite the Beveridge Welfare reforms of 1945 in order to claim they have been misused. Frank is correct that Beveridge was not in favour of means tested benefits on the basis that, on taking up work, loss of benefits meant a massive marginal tax rate that discouraged such working. Coalition policy has attempted in part to overcome this problem but clumsily. However Beveridge's revolution was very definitely based on 'need'. He pointed to squalor, disease and want as well as ignorance and idleness as the 'giant evils'. He was clear that sickness caused worklessness and that poor people could not afford medical attention, creating a vicious circle. He believed that families should be supported at a 'minimum' level for decent living **'for as long as the need lasts'**. This is what he actually said

'The state should not stifle incentive, opportunity, responsibility; in establishing a national minimum [income], it should leave room and encouragement for voluntary action by each individual to provide more than the minimum for himself and his family'.

Who could argue with this? But Beveridge most certainly was about welfare 'meeting need' and 'for as long as it lasts', contrary to Frank's reinterpretation. Beveridge did not advocate starvation level state benefits or using benefits as a weapon of social control.

The story of the targeting of the undeserving poor and vulnerable by the Coalition and rogue Labour MPs like Frank, seemed to go on forever. The author began to wonder just what the silent, 21st century Church stood for. Finally even the Anglican Church, under the new Archbishop Welby, could take no more. The Mission and Public Affairs Council published a remarkable report in June 2013 which is worth comparing with all we have seen about Coalition and New Labour social 'reforms'.

'With material inequality so great, the **moral case** for squeezing welfare recipients is harder to make when the very rich appear to be escaping recession largely unscathed. Unemployment is seen less as a misfortune occasioned by the fluctuating economic cycle and more a **moral matter** reflecting a person's willingness to work. The public debate has very quickly become one about the **deserving and undeserving poor.** Government spokespersons have made political capital out of this and the distinction between **strivers and scroungers has entrenched harsh attitudes** towards those being targeted for cuts. **Where the poor and vulnerable carry a disproportionate share of the burden created by the financial crisis, something is wrong.'**

Amen to that…very wrong indeed. But is Frank's 'Christian' attitude to the undeserving poor really any different from that of the Coalition? By the end of 2014 Frank's dark dream of wholesale state zapping of the feckless poor, via sanctions, was realised. Some 900,000 poor, disabled and sick people had been sanctioned by the Coalition for failing to conform to the Byzantine benefits rules. As Frank's report team told us, this was one, important factor in the rise of UK hunger. At Christmas 2013, Archbishop Welby himself went further.

'No society can be content where misery and want exist unless, through our collective love, we also challenge the greed and selfishness behind them…**Where people are measured in their worth only by what they can produce, what economic value they have, then Christ is denied and our humanity is corrupted.**'

This seems clear enough: whatever the cause of their zero or negative economic value, whether feckless or not, to let such people and their innocent children suffer, is to deny Christ. These words curiously echo those of another churchman from not so long ago.

'We are talking about men and women, our compatriots, our brothers and sisters. Poor, unproductive people if you wish, but does this mean that they have lost their right to live?'

This is from a sermon by Bishop Clemens, Graf von Galen, in 1941, also sent directly to the Fuhrer, protesting the state murder of physically and mentally disabled German adults, under the 'Aktion T4' euthanasia programme. By then all the disabled children of the Reich were dead. This is the point: once people are defined only as economic burdens and even worse, held morally responsible for their own misfortunes, we are on a very slippery slope. The wolf is always lurking just beyond the firelight, waiting for some 'person of authority', some rabid politician, to set it loose and point: there, there is our enemy!

(A personal note: Simply help the poor: that was the understanding in the author's Salvation Army family in one of the poorest areas of Liverpool in the 1950s. My uncle and cousin, good Army men both, went onto the mean streets and did what they could for the poor without discrimination or making moral judgements. I must say, remembering them, his comments on Princess Diana, refugees and much else, Frank's 'brand' of Christianity is not one that I recognise.)

We began by looking at Frank's Feeding Britain report. Let's end with his comments on Feeding Birkenhead, made to the Wirral Globe in January 2015

'We're bringing together our churches, charities, schools and supermarkets to get food to those in need and, **as importantly to use this as a way of beginning to deal with the major problems in people's lives**'

Yes, the inadequate and undeserving poor will be sent to the ineffective, sanctions based, Troubled Families Projects where their real intellectual and medical problems will still not be addressed, whatever the hype. In the 21st century, hunger is still apparently a weapon that can be wielded covertly (remembering Lady Jenkin's 'porridge' faux pas) to reshape society into one's own ideological image …unless we are vigilant and stop it.

Let us review what we have learned. From all we have shared of Frank's own words in Neighbours From Hell it is clear that Frank helped build the New Labour ASBO Jihad which 'sexed up' fear of crime, disorder and 'low level terrorism', as Blair called it, and criminalised the mentally disordered, including children. Frank then exploited this populist political artefact to promote his model of an authoritarian, ordered society with its roots in his view of evangelical Christianity, with the backdrop of the Poor Laws, workhouses and treadmills of Victorian England.

Of course the ASBO Jihad was a failure. It did not protect the public but it did criminalise many thousands of mentally disordered children and adults who needed medical help. But it also showed a control freak government how far it could go in dismantling ancient legal protections, essential to all of us, by concentrating at first on unpopular minorities and turning them into folk devils. Nor did the 'ASBO Sin Bins' successfully re-programme the chaotic, troubled, 'families from hell'. They merely put targets on their backs for the local vigilantes.

The Coalition has adopted the same approach with a vengeance…now even the 'deserving poor' had better watch out.

It is also clear that Frank is completely, indeed fanatically, sincere in his social and religious views and he has the right to express them just as we, hopefully, still have the right to test, debate and reject them; although if Frank had his way we would not be allowed to do this.

We have also seen that Frank's views on the undeserving poor and dysfunctional families have not changed over the years.

The content of his Feeding Britain report makes it clear that he is still in part, blaming the victims for being inadequate …and morally degenerate. He is still trying to sell his Moral Jihad to any political party that might listen. It would be a dangerous mistake to see Frank merely as a slightly eccentric, aging MP with an axe to grind: as a kind of principled, 'holy fool' of little relevance. Although Frank's major reviews of welfare and poverty were publicly rejected, they and his other works represent a treasure trove of ready made, sometimes extreme ideas, moralistic justifications and sanctions based interventions, which governments can dip into for tactical political benefit as the times and the public mood allow.

It is a pity, on the local scene, that the mainly poor electorate of Birkenhead will no doubt continue, thanks to his populist rhetoric, to see Uncle Frank as their friend, or at least, sleepwalk into a Labour vote in the false hope of deliverance from poverty and want. Frank has been their MP since 1979, including a thirteen year stretch under powerful, New Labour governments. They should ask themselves why 55% of them are still reliant on out of work benefits, or are they all undeserving scroungers? They should also recall that Frank wants to bring back Citizen's Contracts and National Service for the unemployed like them, in order to restore

'a sense of **order and patriotism**'

After all, according to Frank, his constituency is now like 'Beirut' …despite all the legislation Frank has proposed in Parliament, all the coercive law he has supported, and all his puffed up, media rhetoric over twenty five years. Why get fooled again?

It was remarkable how many times, when things were bad for them, that the New Labour government played the 'antisocial behaviour' and 'scrounger' cards. We can similarly expect the Coalition and the next government to dip into Frank's box of sanctions as austerity trundles on, including their moralistic justification based on the supposedly shameful and irresponsible behaviour of the feckless poor. (See recent speeches by Eric Pickles, the Coalition C&LG minister for examples).

We must be alert to this kind of 'fear and hate spin' based policy so often used successfully by populist politicians to sell their extreme ideological visions, or to merely divert public attention from their failings. Historically it has all too often ended badly for everybody involved. We should recall Frank's warning at the beginning of this essay about totalitarian regimes and note that of another famous expert

'The people can always be brought to the bidding of the leader. That is easy. All you have to do is tell them they are being attacked and denounce the pacifists for lack of patriotism…'

Reich Marshal Herman Goring; Nuremberg Trials, 1945.

When a supposedly 'moral' dimension underlies such a political strategy, as Archbishop Welby has observed, things can become even worse. I will end with the famous warning of the great Christian writer, C S Lewis

'It may be better to live under robber barons than under **omnipotent moral busybodies.** The robber barons may sometimes sleep but those who torment us for our own good will torment us without end for they do so with the approval of their consciences'

Frank Field: omnipotent moral busybody, dangerous fruitcake, or saintly friend of the poor? You decide.

Professor D P Gregg (retired)

February 2015

Bibliography

'Neighbours from Hell', Frank Field MP; Politico's, 2003

See also www. frankfield.com

'Taking Liberties', Chris Atkins, et al; Revolver Books, 2007

'Family Intervention Projects: a classic case of policy based evidence'; David P Gregg; Centre for Crime & Justice Studies; Evidence Based Policy Series; 2010

'CHAVS', Owen Jones, Verso, 2012

'The ASBO Gestapo', David P Gregg; Green Man Books, 2014